Let's Look at the Seasons

Summertime

By Ann Schweninger

VIKING

The art was prepared with graphite pencil,
colored pencil, and watercolor paint on Arches
90-pound cold-press watercolor paper.

VIKING
Published by the Penguin Group
Viking Penguin, a division of Penguin Books USA Inc.,
375 Hudson Street, New York, New York 10014, U.S.A.
Penguin Books Ltd, 27 Wrights Lane, London W8 5TZ, England
Penguin Books Australia Ltd, Ringwood, Victoria, Australia
Penguin Books Canada Ltd, 10 Alcorn Avenue, Toronto, Ontario, Canada M4V 3B2
Penguin Books (N.Z.) Ltd, 182–190 Wairau Road, Auckland 10, New Zealand

Penguin Books Ltd, Registered Offices: Harmondsworth, Middlesex, England

First published in 1992 by Viking Penguin, a division of Penguin Books USA Inc.

1   3   5   7   9   10   8   6   4   2

Library of Congress Cataloging-in-Publication Data
Schweninger, Ann. Summertime / by Ann Schweninger.
p.   cm.—(Let's look at the seasons)
Summary: Explores the changes that happen in nature during the summer.
I S B N   0 - 6 7 0 - 8 3 6 1 0 - 9   :
1. Summer—Juvenile literature.   2. Science—Miscellanea—
Juvenile literature. [1. Summer. 2. Nature.]   I. Title.
II. Series: Schweninger, Ann. Let's look at the seasons.
QB637.6.S38   1992 574.5′43—dc20   91-33030   CIP   AC

Printed in Hong Kong   Set in ITC Cheltenham Light

For Hunter

First Day

The first day of summer
is usually June 21st.
The sun rises earlier,
and sets later, than on
any other day of the year.

Early Summer

This is a time of growth. For animals, food is plentiful.

A deer eats lots of grass. Her fawns nip at grass shoots. But mostly they nurse, drinking her milk.

Mother mallard ducks and their ducklings eat tiny weeds, little seeds, and small insects they find in the water.

Painted turtles sun themselves on a log. In the water, they find fish, tadpoles, insects, worms, and weeds to eat.

Frogs catch insects, worms, and snails on the tips of their tongues!

Hummingbirds, butterflies, and bees sip nectar from blossom centers. A fine yellow powder inside the flower, called pollen, collects on their bodies. As they move from blossom to blossom, it rubs off onto one flower of the same kind, then another, and another. The pollen moves down into the blossom's center and then, slowly, the blossom becomes a seed . . . or many seeds.

Garden Flowers

| daylily | pansy | sweet pea | rose |

This process is called pollination. Without it, flowers would not develop seeds and new flowers could not grow.

Sometimes the wind carries pollen from one flower to another.

And some plants can pollinate themselves. Pollen from one part of the blossom rubs off onto its center, so this flower, too, will become a seed.

Wildflowers

dandelion

red clover

buttercup

oxeye daisy

July Fun

Summer Tree

A tree is growing. Its trunk grows taller. Its branches grow longer.

Many new leaves are growing, too.

Roots grow. They reach into the soil and bring minerals and water to the tree.

Leaves make food for the tree with sunlight and gases from the air, and minerals and water from the soil.

Monarch Butterfly

A tiny egg has been laid on the leaf of a milkweed plant.

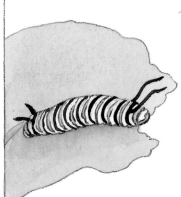

In about four days, a caterpillar hatches from the egg. For about ten days, it munches milkweed leaves. Then . . .

new skin

. . . it hangs upside-down. From inside its skin, a new skin grows. The new skin is tough and hard.

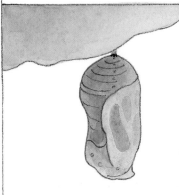

The old skin falls off. The caterpillar has become a pupa.

In about twelve days, the pupa opens and a butterfly emerges. It waits for its delicate wings to dry.

Then into the air it flutters!

Heat Wave

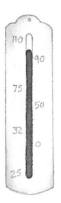

It's hot!

When you go outside:

Wear sunscreen to protect your skin, sunglasses or a visor to protect your eyes, and a hat to cover your head.

If you feel very hot, dizzy, tired, weak, sick to your stomach, or have a headache or cramps, you may have heat stroke or heat exhaustion. Tell an adult and get to a cool place right away. You may need to see a doctor.

Play outside in the early morning and in the evening, when it is coolest. Try to stay in the shade. Drink plenty of liquids. And don't let yourself get too hot!

Thunderstorm

Big billows of clouds fill the sky. Warm moist air rushes upward from the earth. High above, inside clouds, the moisture cools and condenses onto tiny dust particles, becoming thousands of raindrops. The raindrops begin to fall. But warm air from the earth still rushes upward, whipping raindrops inside clouds up and down, up and down!

Rising and falling raindrops create so much friction that strong electrical currents build up, then strike. Lightning!

Lightning is so hot and affects air around it so suddenly that it creates a loud sound. Thunder!

Thunderstorm Safety Tips

• The safest place to be is inside a house or other large building.

• If you are caught outside, lie down flat on the ground and stay there until the storm is over.

• If you are inside a car, stay there.

• Don't seek shelter under a tree or small structure like a telephone booth, or in any small structure in an open area.

• Don't go near telephone wires, TV antennas, or carry an umbrella.

• Don't swim, boat, or take a bath or shower.

Making Ice Pops

Here's what you need:

 fruit juice

 an ice-cube tray

 wooden sticks

Pour the fruit juice into an ice-cube tray.

Put a wooden stick into each section of the tray.

Place the ice-cube tray in the freezer. It will take about four hours for the juice to freeze.

When it's time, take the tray out. (Careful, it's cold! Use potholders.) Remove the ice pops. And enjoy!

Beach Time

The beach is a favorite place to visit for a summer weekend or vacation.

Beach Safety Tips

• Be careful not to get sunburned. On the beach, sit in the shade of an umbrella.

• You can become sunburned even in the water. Put sunscreen on before and after you swim.

• Swim only when an adult and a lifeguard are nearby.

Nighttime

The sky is full of stars. Look toward the northern sky. Can you see a constellation of stars shaped like a pan with a handle? It's called the Big Dipper.

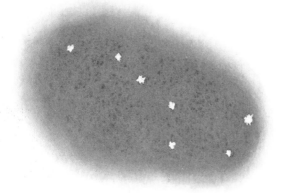

A shooting star, also called a falling star, is really a meteorite burning up as it enters the earth's atmosphere. When you see one, make a wish!

East of the Rocky Mountains, you will see twinkling lights on the lawn and in the trees. These are small insects called fireflies or lightning bugs.

August Gardens

This is a lush time in the garden. Seeds planted in the spring have grown all summer. Now it's time to harvest.

We eat plant leaves.

lettuce

spinach

We eat stems.

rhubarb

We eat roots.

beets

carrots

We eat fruit.

tomatoes

melon

We eat vegetables.

squash

cauliflower

We eat seeds.

corn

August Fun

Let's count the days until school begins. One, two, three, four, five. . .

Late Summer Seeds

Summer wind blows dandelion seeds away to new places. Winter rain and snow bury the seeds in soil; when spring arrives, they will grow.

A squirrel buries an acorn and then forgets to dig it up to eat during the winter. In the spring, the acorn will grow into an oak tree seedling.

Bur marigold seeds catch on pant legs and animals' fur. Pulled off and dropped to the ground, the seeds will grow in the spring.

We harvest seeds from vegetables, grain, fruit, and flowers. We save the seeds until it is springtime, then plant them in a garden or field.

Birds eat berries, and the seeds inside fall to the ground with the birds' droppings. Then, in spring, new berry bushes grow.

Pine-tree seeds are tucked inside pinecones. When pinecones open, seeds fall to the ground. In springtime, new pine trees begin to grow.

September

As summer ends, rose and buttercup blossoms fade, and goldenrod and aster blossoms bloom.

Baby animals have been growing all summer and are almost as big as their parents. They will be ready for cold weather when it comes.

Young birds have learned to fly. Some will stay during the cold time ahead. Many more take off, flying south for the winter.